Interiors Rooms to Color

By Beth Ingrias

Want to color more for FREE?

Get a FREE 25 page adult coloring book

visit

www.BethIngrias.com

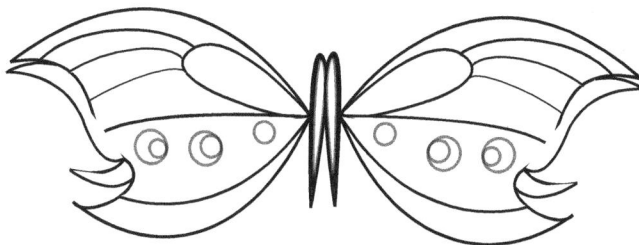

ISBN-13: 978-1-945803-09-3
ISBN-10: 1-945803-09-6

A Sample of What's Inside

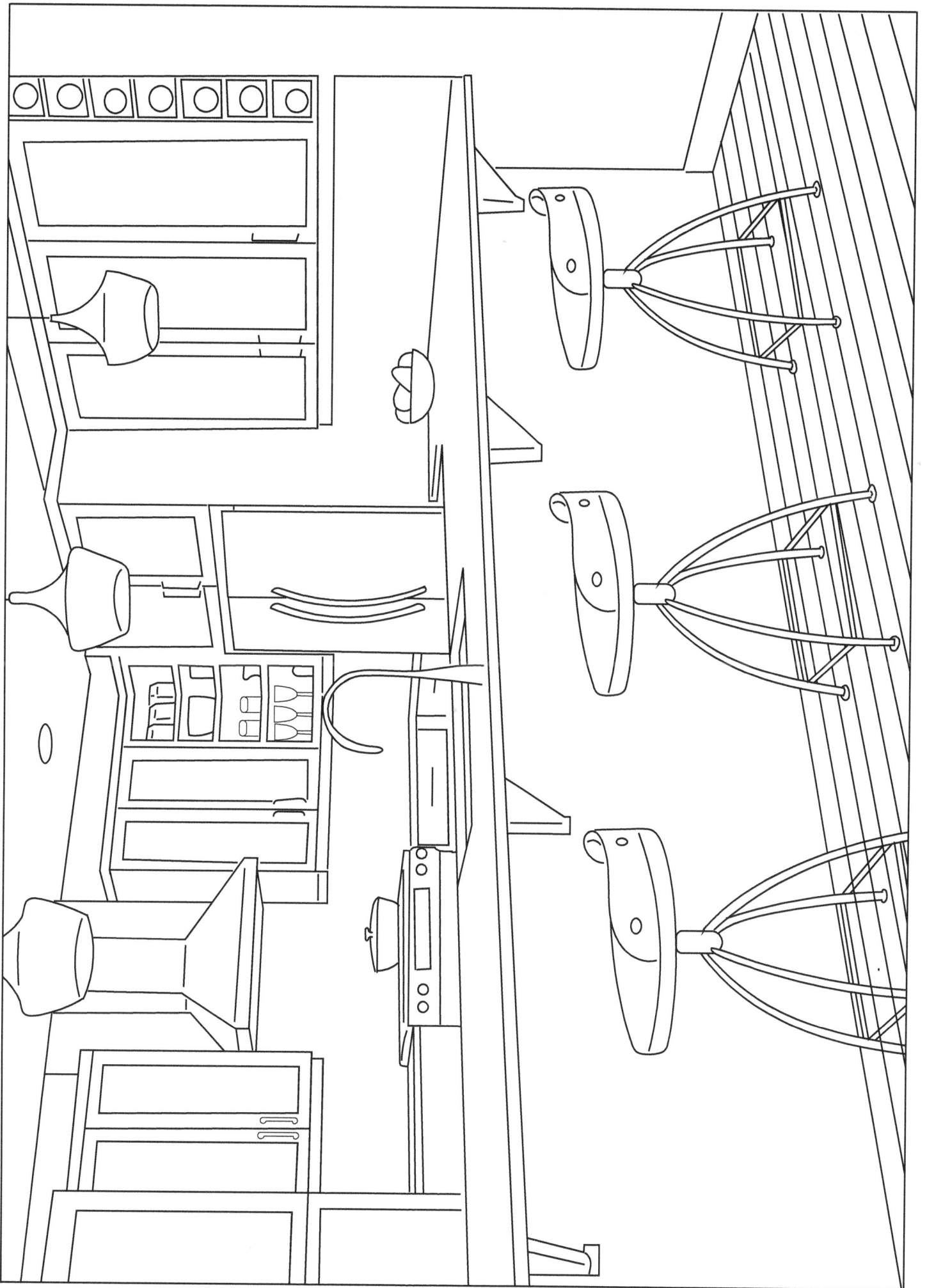

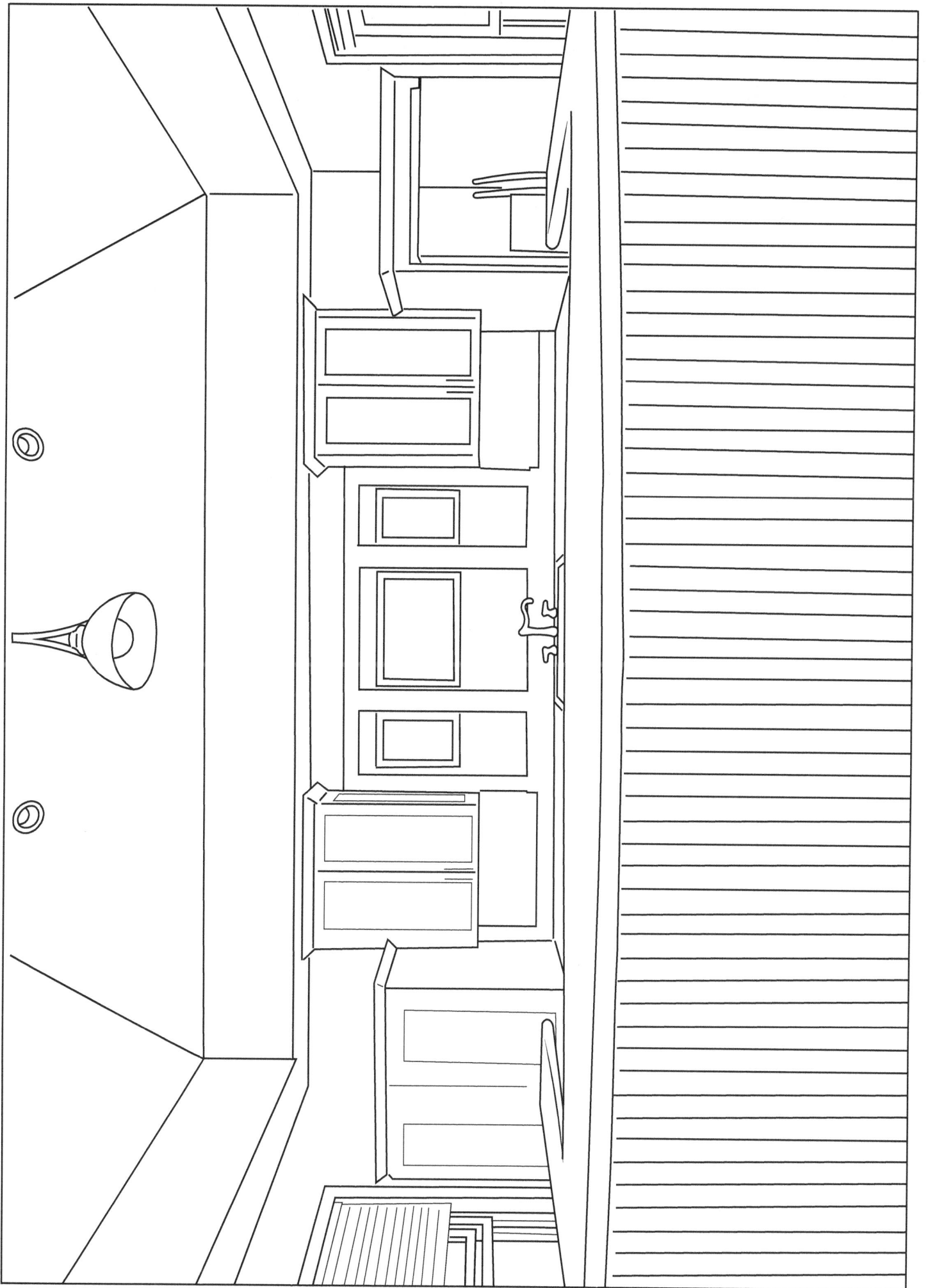

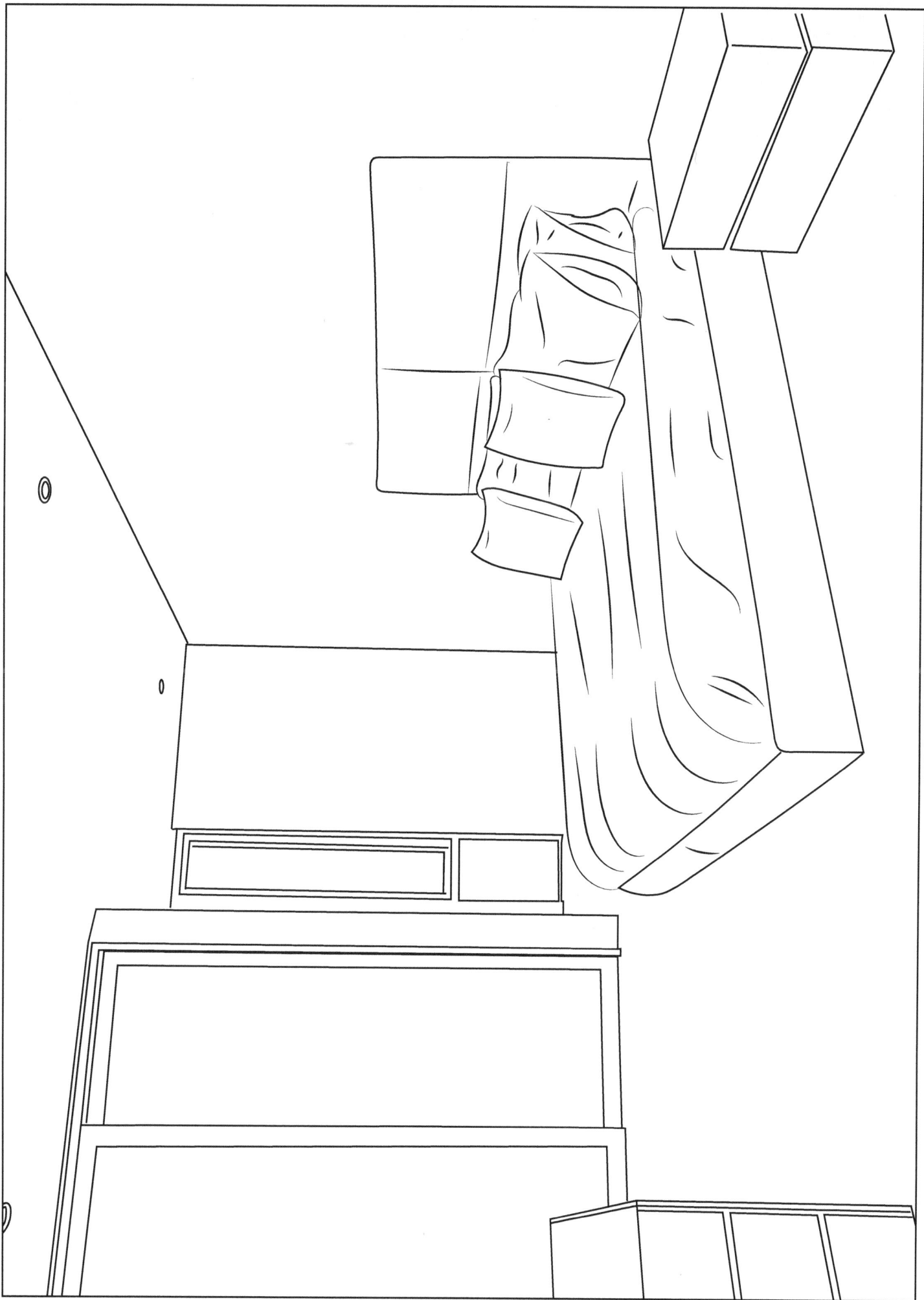

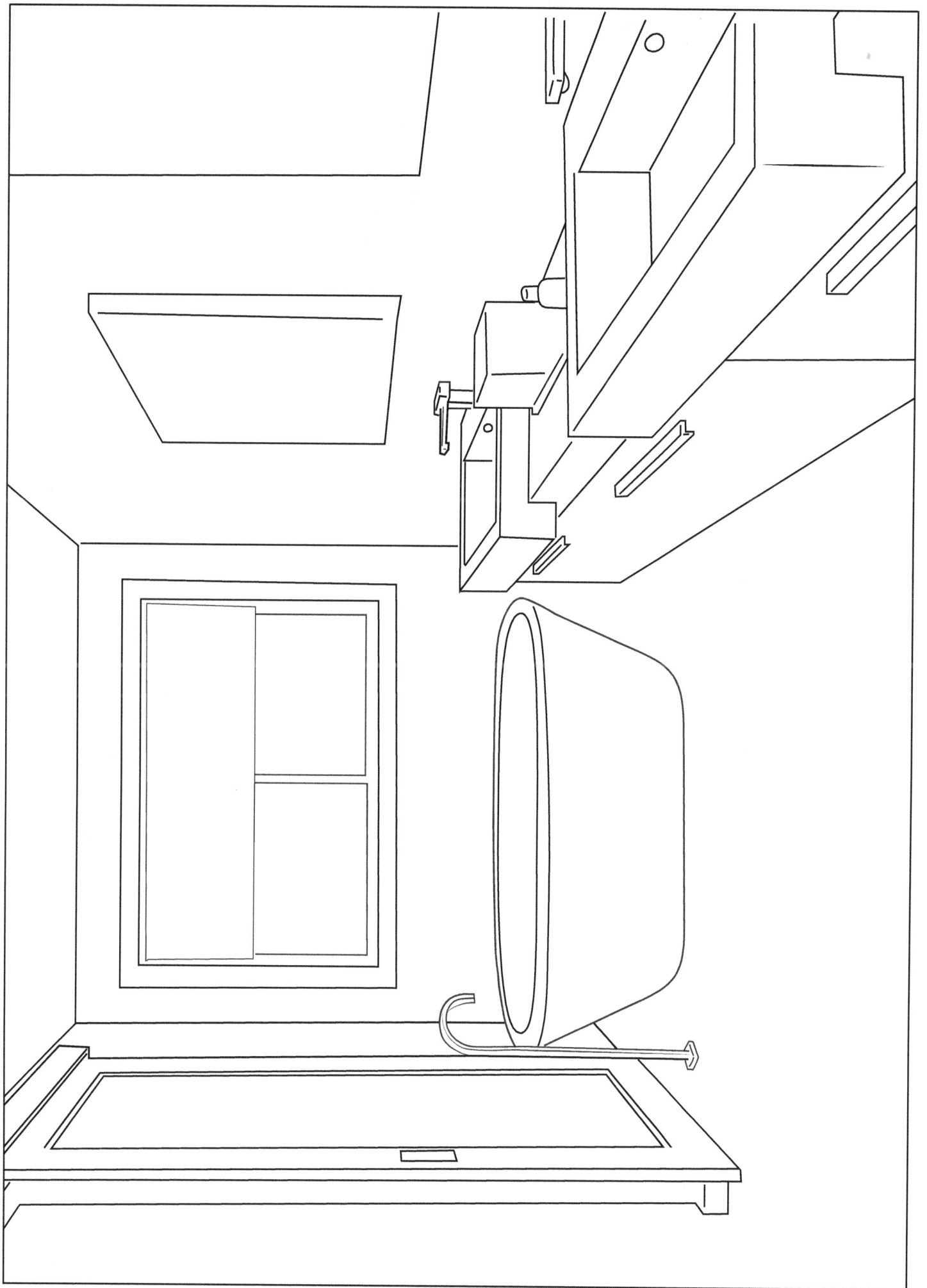

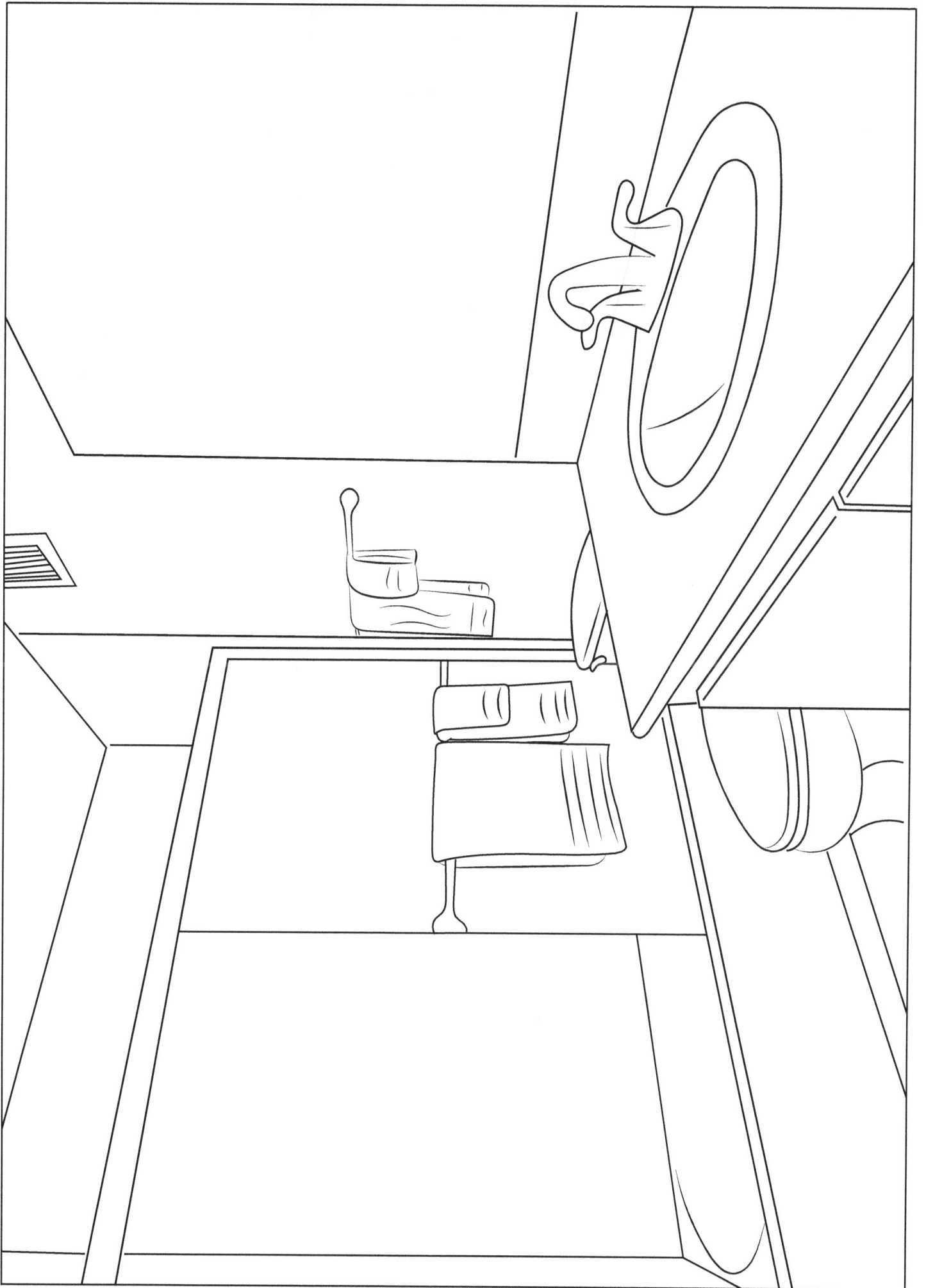

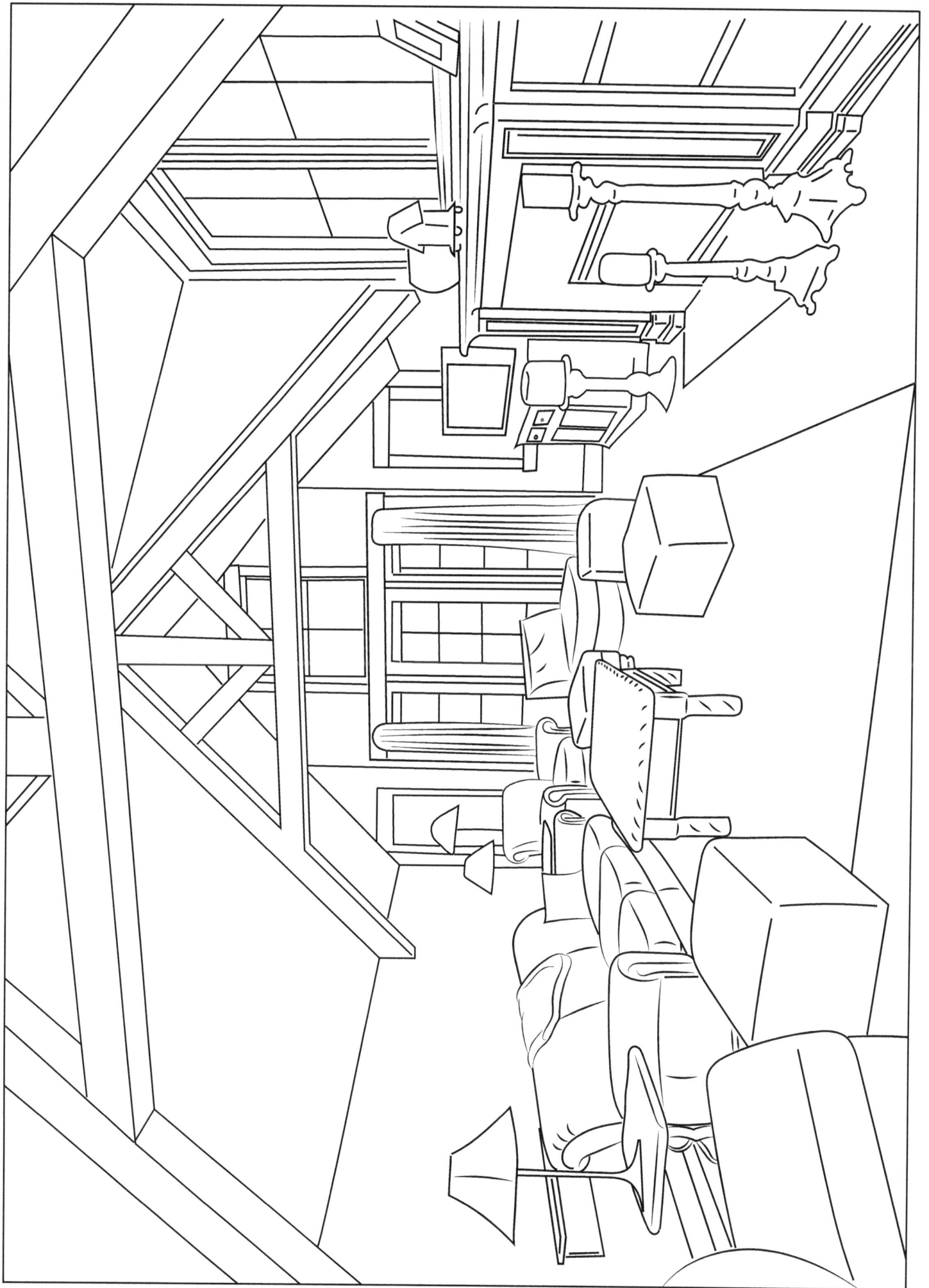

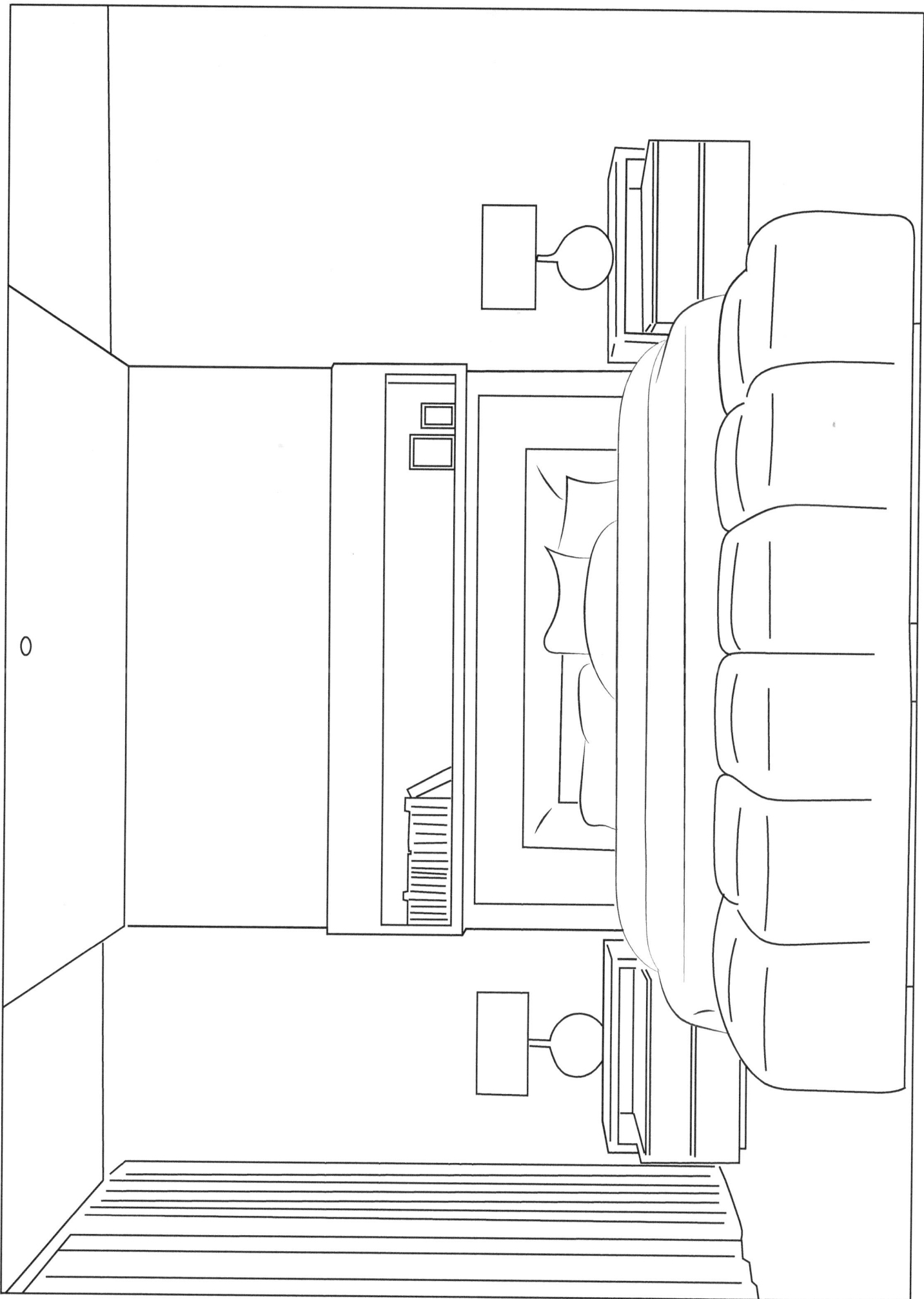

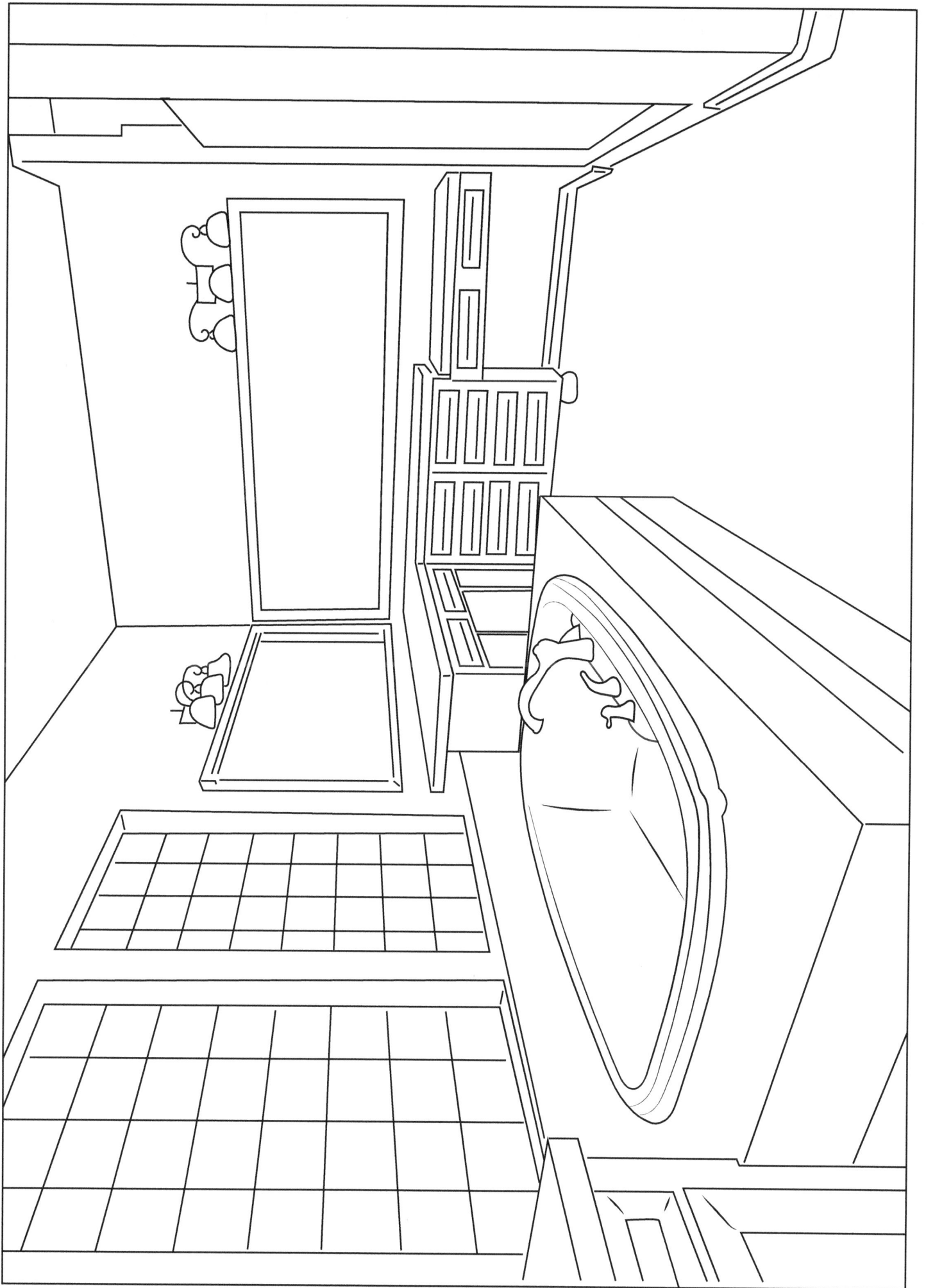

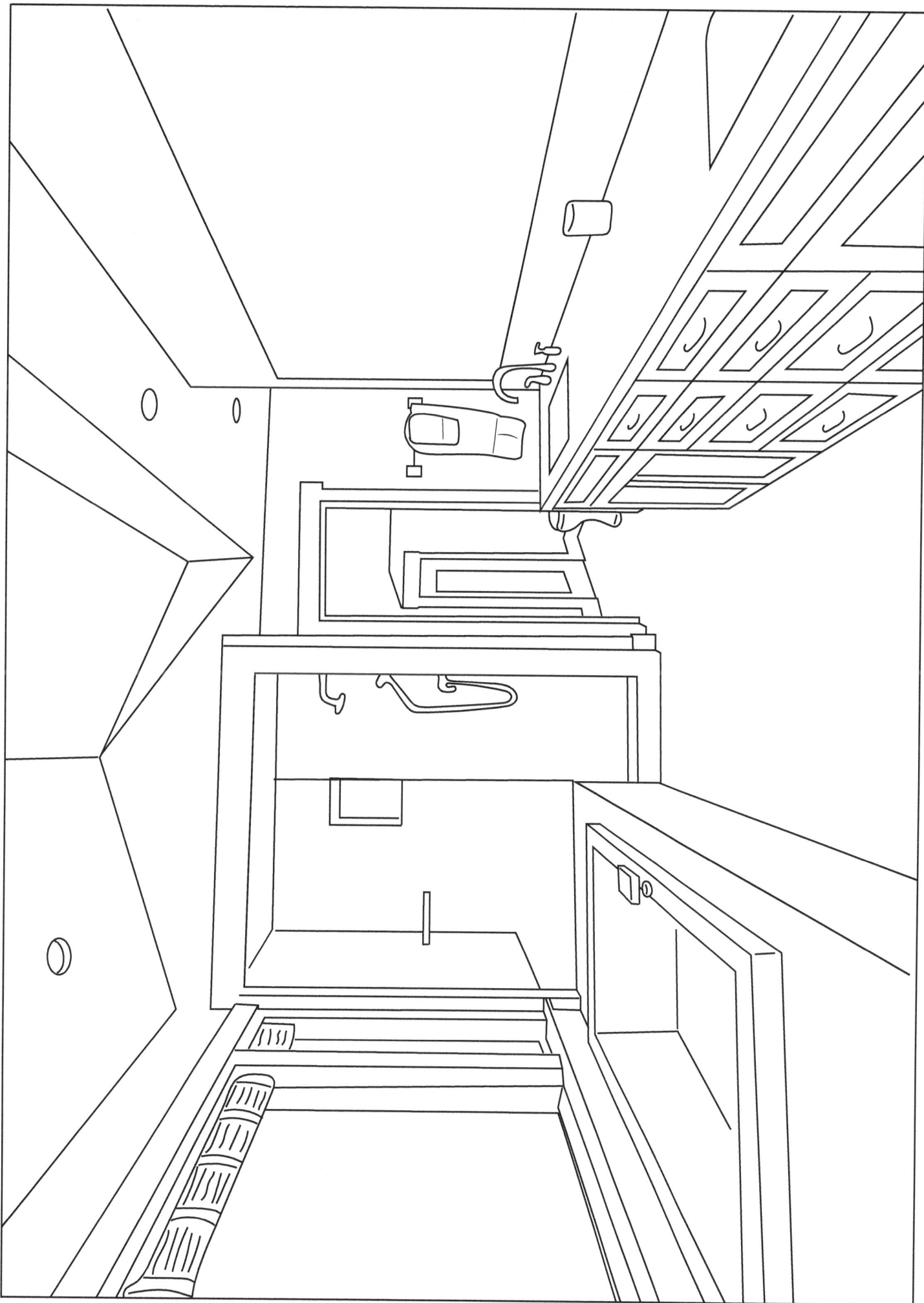

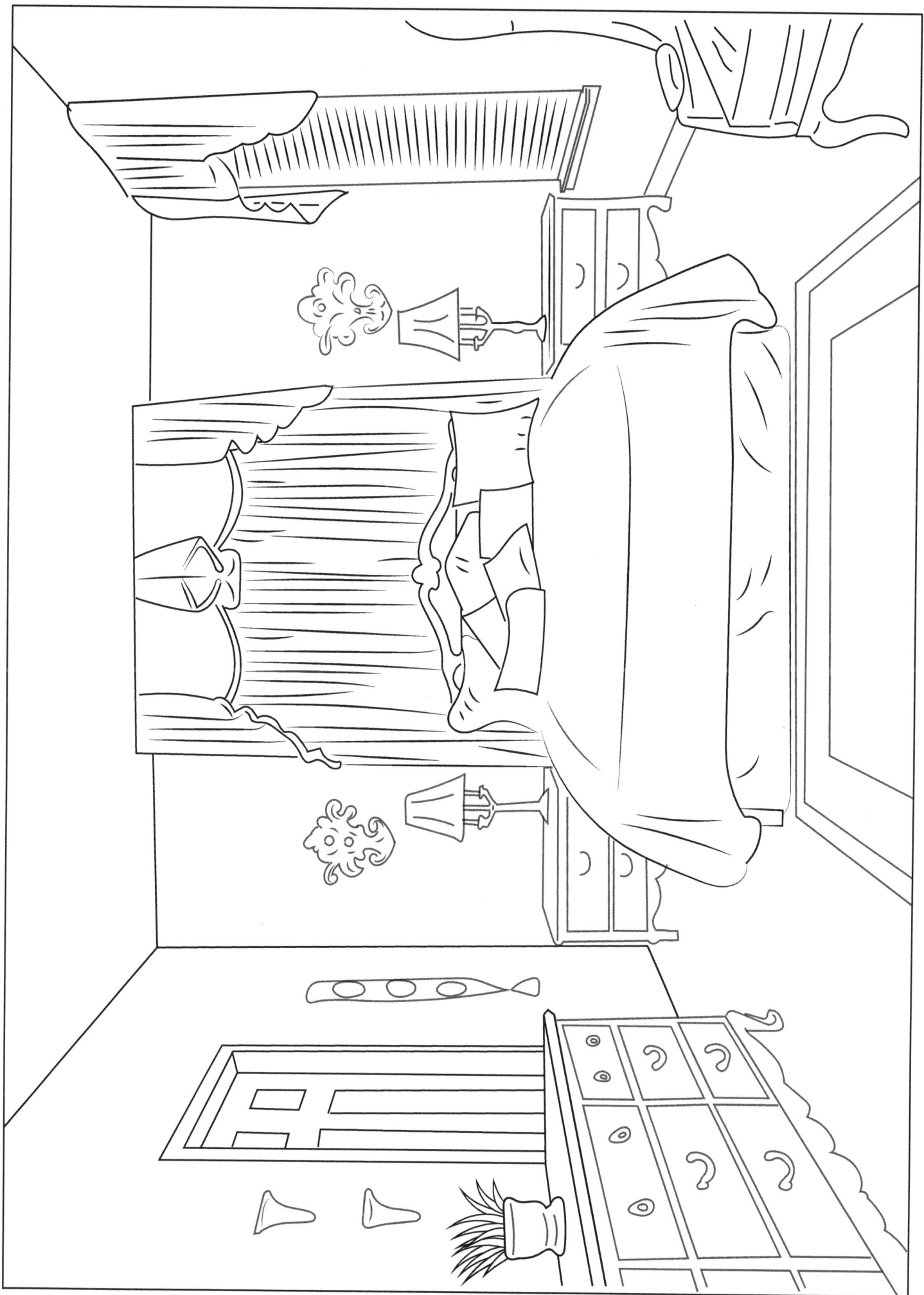

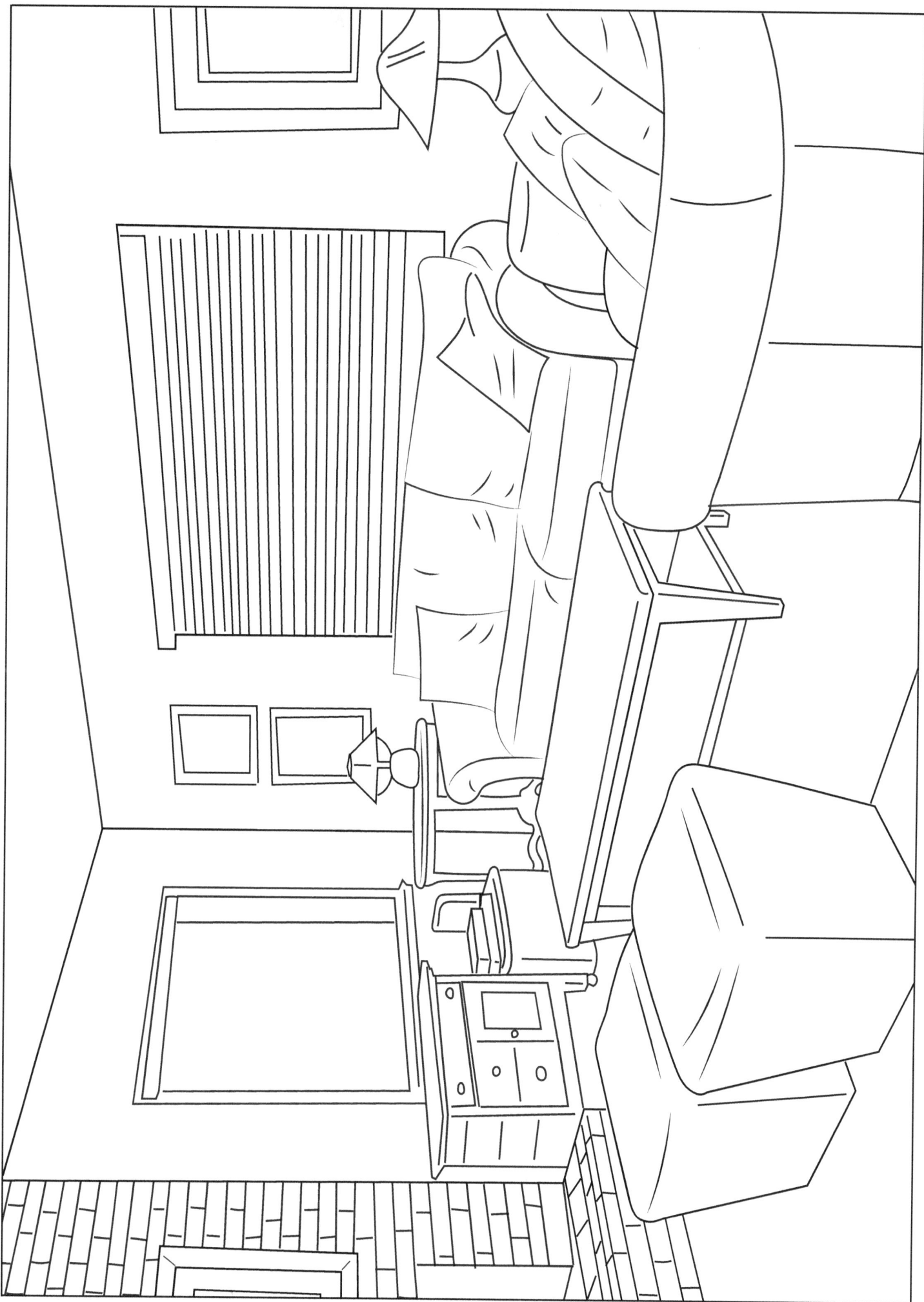

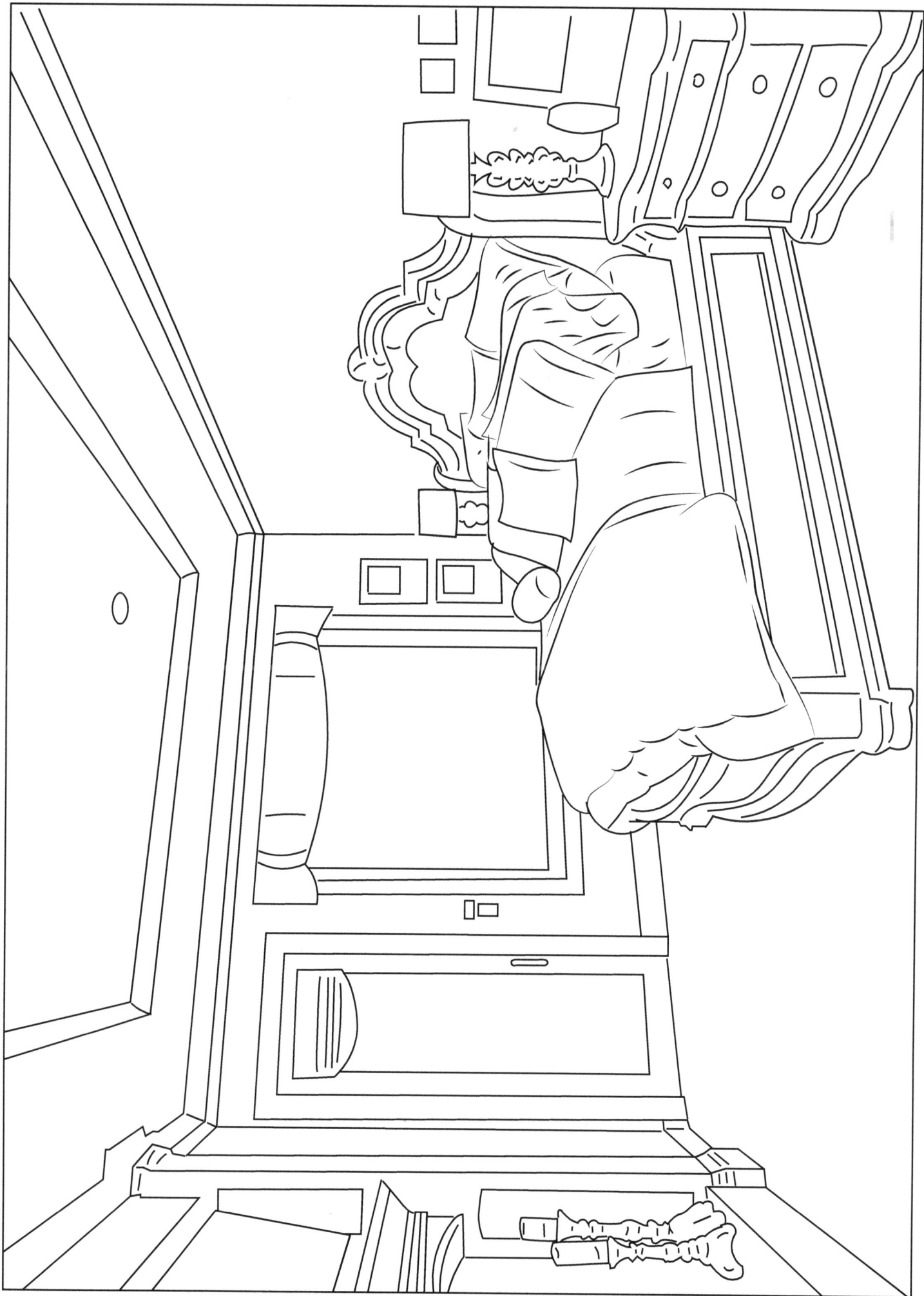

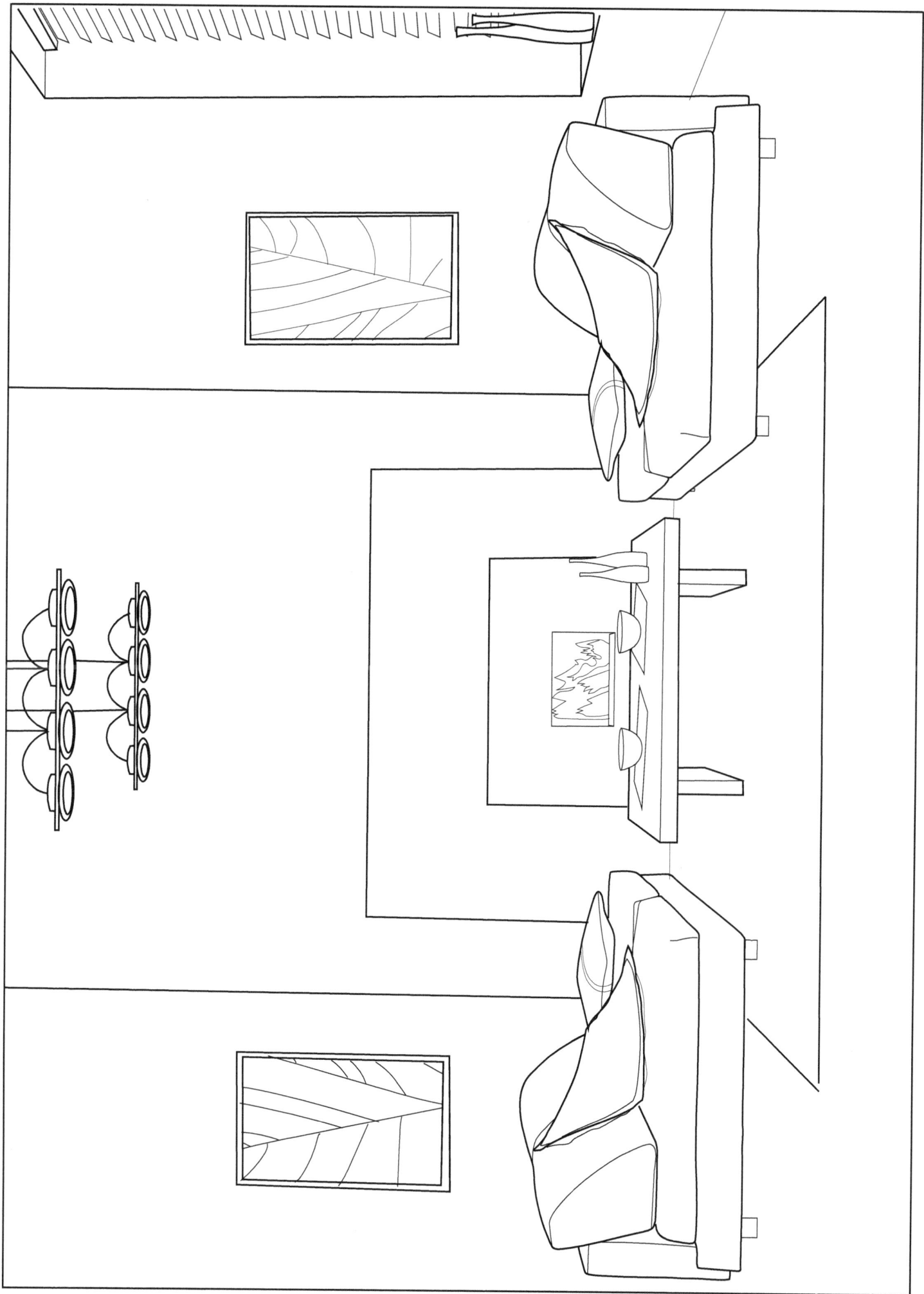

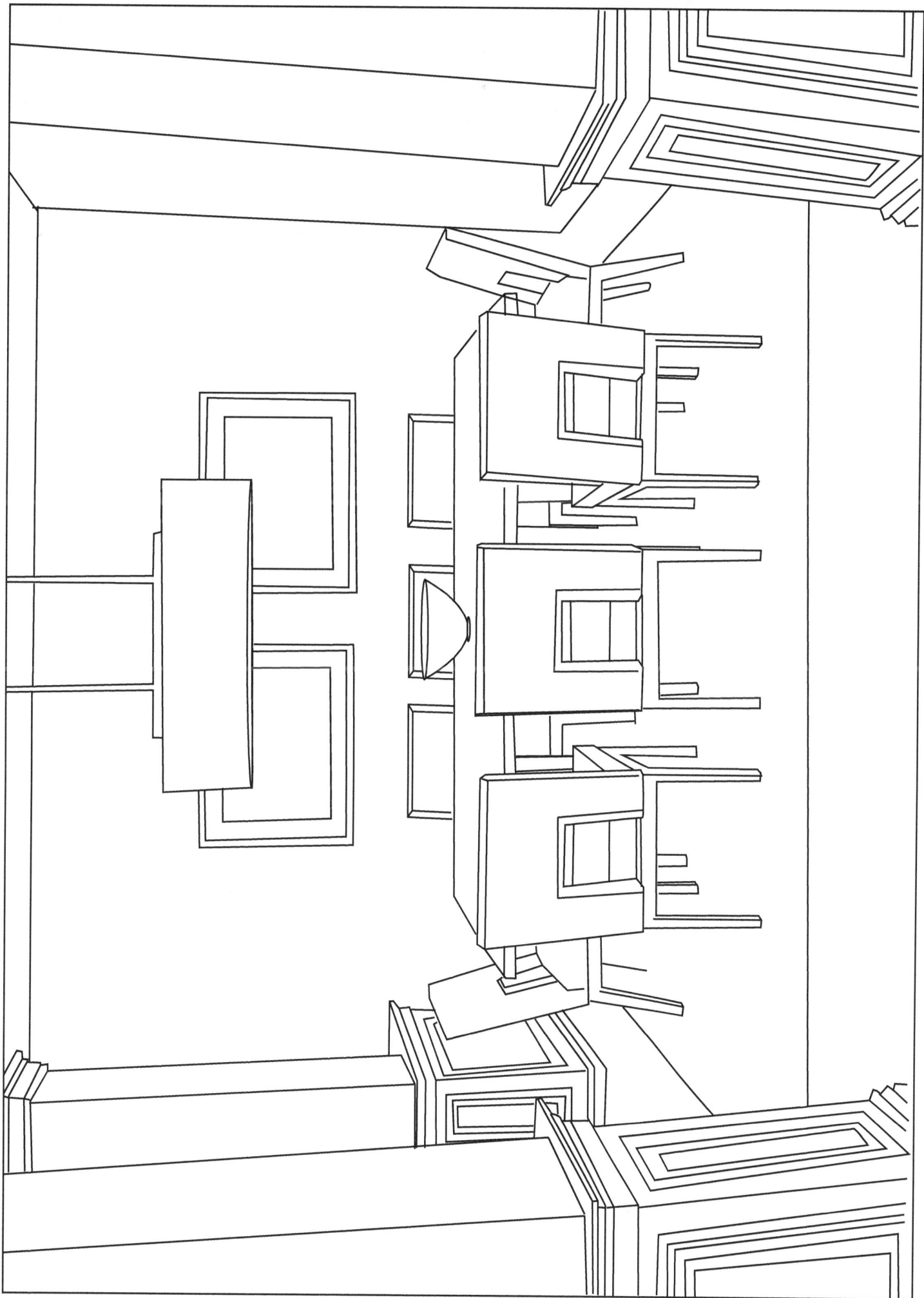

Thanks for picking up a copy of my book. I really appreciate it. If you enjoyed coloring these pages please feel free to leave a review! I would love to hear what you think of my designs.

I would also love to see how you have chosen to color some of my designs. Feel free to email me some pictures of the pages you have colored. You can email me here:

bethingrias@gmail.com

Thanks,
Beth

P.S.
Don't forget to get your free 25 page coloring book at my website.

www.bethingrias.com

www.ingramcontent.com/pod-product-compliance
Lightning Source LLC
Chambersburg PA
CBHW081251040426
42452CB00015B/2792